Entrepreneurial Mindset:

Do YOU Have What It Takes?

Liane Pinel

Copyright 2023 Liane Pinel -All Rights Reserved
Open Eyes Publishing
A Division of
Liane Pinel Consulting

Entrepreneurial Mindset: Do YOU Have What It Takes?

Table of Contents:

1. The Call of Entrepreneurship

2. Nurturing the Seed of an Idea

3. Embracing the Risk: Overcoming Fear and Doubt

4. The Power of Connection: Effective Communication and Networking for Entrepreneurship

5. Mastering Time Management: Boosting Productivity for Entrepreneurial Success

6. Unleashing Creativity: The Power of Innovation and Adaptability

7. The Power of Resilience: Bouncing Back and Thriving in Adversity

8. Decisive Action: Making Informed Decisions and Solving Problems with Confidence

9. Leading with Inspiration: Building a High-Performing Team for Collective Success

10. Embracing Adaptability: Navigating Change and Thriving in a Dynamic Business Landscape

11. The Power of Connection: Effective Communication and Relationship-Building for Entrepreneurial Success

12. Lifelong Learning: Fueling Growth and Adapting to a Changing Business Landscape

---

Book Introduction:

Welcome to "Entrepreneurial Mindset: Do YOU Have What It Takes?" In this book, we will embark on a journey of self-discovery and exploration to determine if you possess the qualities and mindset required to thrive as an entrepreneur.

Liane Pinel is a serial entrepreneur, an author, artist, photographer, designer, business and life coach and the Founder of The Spirit Within Canada. With over 40 years of business experience and 25 years as an entrepreneur and coach, Liane guides others to follow their hearts and make an impact in the world with their businesses. Whether you're an aspiring entrepreneur or already running your own business, this book will provide valuable insights, practical advice, and inspiring stories to help you unlock your full potential.

Being an entrepreneur is not just about starting a business; it's a way of life. It requires a unique set of skills, traits, and perspectives that set you apart from the crowd. In the following chapters, we will delve into various aspects of the entrepreneurial mindset, equipping you with the tools you need to succeed in the competitive world of business.

Throughout this book, we will adopt an optimistic tone, celebrating the boundless opportunities that come with entrepreneurship. We will encourage you to embrace your passion, take calculated risks, and learn from both successes and failures. This book is not a roadmap to instant success, but rather a guide to developing the right mindset and attitude for long-term entrepreneurial fulfillment.

Whether you dream of launching a startup, scaling your business, or simply want to cultivate an entrepreneurial mindset in your professional and personal life, this book is for you. So, grab a pen and notebook, get comfortable, and let's dive into the captivating world of entrepreneurship!

Chapter 1: The Call of Entrepreneurship

Imagine a life where you have the freedom to pursue your dreams, the ability to make a real impact, and the opportunity to shape your own destiny. This is the call of entrepreneurship—a beckoning that resonates with individuals who yearn for something more than the conventional nine-to-five grind. In this chapter, we will explore the allure of entrepreneurship, the characteristics of successful entrepreneurs, and the first steps you can take to answer the call.

Entrepreneurship is not for the faint of heart, but for those willing to embark on this exciting journey, the rewards can be tremendous. We'll discuss the advantages of working for yourself, including the potential for financial independence, creative fulfillment, and the ability to build something meaningful from scratch. We'll also touch on the challenges and sacrifices that come with the entrepreneurial path, helping you understand the realities and prepare mentally for the road ahead.

Throughout this chapter, we will emphasize the importance of self-reflection. By examining your passions, strengths, and values, you can gain a deeper understanding of whether entrepreneurship aligns with your aspirations and purpose. We'll provide practical exercises and thought-provoking questions to guide you in this introspective process.

Remember, entrepreneurship is not just about starting a business; it's a mindset and a way of life. So, let's begin this exciting exploration and discover if you have what it takes to embrace the entrepreneurial journey!

Picture yourself waking up every morning with a sense of purpose and excitement, knowing that you have the power to shape your day according to your vision. No more clock-watching or waiting for the weekend. As an entrepreneur, you have the freedom to set your own schedule, pursue your passions, and make a positive impact on the world.

One of the key traits that successful entrepreneurs possess is a burning desire to create something meaningful. They have an insatiable hunger to bring their ideas to life and solve problems that matter. They see opportunities where others see obstacles, and they have an unwavering belief in their ability to make a difference. If you find yourself nodding along to these descriptions, then you might just have the entrepreneurial fire within you.

However, it's essential to understand that entrepreneurship is not all sunshine and rainbows. It requires hard work, dedication, and a willingness to step outside your comfort zone. You'll face challenges, setbacks, and moments of doubt along the way. But here's the beauty of it: every obstacle you overcome will make you stronger, more resilient, and more confident in your abilities.

In this chapter, we'll help you assess your entrepreneurial readiness. We'll guide you through a series of questions and exercises designed to unlock your entrepreneurial potential. Remember, this is not about judging whether you're "cut out" for entrepreneurship or not. It's about self-discovery and understanding your strengths, weaknesses, and areas of growth. You might surprise yourself with hidden talents and untapped potential.

As we delve into the world of entrepreneurship, let go of any preconceived notions or limiting beliefs. Embrace the possibility that you have within you the power to create something extraordinary. Even if you don't have all the answers right now, that's perfectly fine. This book is your roadmap to self-discovery and personal growth.

Are you ready to embark on this exhilarating journey? Are you prepared to challenge yourself, learn new skills, and embrace the uncertainty that comes with entrepreneurship? If your heart is racing with anticipation, then let's dive into Chapter 1: The Call of Entrepreneurship and discover the extraordinary possibilities that lie ahead.

Section 1: The Allure of Entrepreneurship

Have you ever found yourself daydreaming about a life where you're in control of your destiny? A life where you can pursue your passions, follow your own path, and make a meaningful impact on the world? That's the allure of entrepreneurship—the irresistible call that beckons those who dare to dream big.

Entrepreneurship offers a unique opportunity for personal and professional growth. It allows you to escape the confines of traditional employment and create a life on your terms. But what is it that makes entrepreneurship so captivating? Let's explore some of the most enticing aspects.

1. Freedom and Autonomy:

    As an entrepreneur, you have the freedom to set your own schedule, work on projects that align with your values, and make decisions without having to go through layers of bureaucracy. You have the autonomy to shape your business and your life according to your vision.

2. Creative Expression:

    Entrepreneurship is a canvas where you can unleash your creativity. It's an outlet for your ideas, innovation, and unique perspectives. You have the opportunity to bring something new and exciting into the world, whether it's a product, a service, or an entire business model.

3. Impact and Significance:

    Many entrepreneurs are driven by the desire to make a difference. They want to solve pressing problems, improve lives, and leave a lasting legacy. When you work for yourself, you have the power to create meaningful change in the lives of others and contribute to the greater good.

4. Flexibility and Work-Life Balance:

   Being an entrepreneur allows you to design a lifestyle that suits your needs and priorities. You can find a balance between work and personal life, allowing you to spend quality time with loved ones, pursue hobbies, and take care of your well-being. It's about creating a harmonious integration of work and life that brings you joy and fulfillment.

5. Financial Independence:

   While entrepreneurship comes with risks, it also offers the potential for financial independence. When you build a successful business, you have the opportunity to reap the rewards of your hard work. You can create wealth, generate passive income, and achieve a level of financial stability that may not be attainable through traditional employment.

6. Continuous Learning and Growth:

   As an entrepreneur, every day is a chance to learn something new. You'll face challenges that push you out of your comfort zone, forcing you to acquire new skills, expand your knowledge, and develop a growth mindset. The journey of entrepreneurship is a never-ending quest for personal and professional growth.

7. Fulfilling Your Purpose:

   Entrepreneurship allows you to align your work with your purpose. It's about pursuing a venture that resonates deeply with your values, passions, and strengths. When you have a sense of purpose, your work becomes more meaningful, fulfilling, and inspiring. It gives you a sense of direction and a reason to wake up excited every morning.

Now that we've explored the allure of entrepreneurship, let's take a moment to reflect on your own aspirations. What is it about entrepreneurship that appeals to you? What are your personal reasons for considering this path? Take a deep breath and let your imagination soar. Envision the life you desire, the impact you want to make, and the fulfillment you seek.

Remember, the call of entrepreneurship is not reserved for a select few. It's a call that resonates with anyone willing to embrace the challenges, nurture their creativity, and pursue their dreams. As we continue our journey through this book, we'll uncover the qualities and mindset required to thrive as an entrepreneur.

In the upcoming sections of this chapter, we'll explore the characteristics of successful entrepreneurs and the first steps you can take to answer the call. Get ready to discover your entrepreneurial potential, unleash your inner innovator, and embark on a transformative adventure.

Are you excited? I know I am! Let's dive into Section 2: Characteristics of Successful Entrepreneurs and unravel the mysteries of what sets them apart from the crowd. Get ready to unleash your entrepreneurial spirit and discover the true depths of your capabilities.

Section 2: Characteristics of Successful Entrepreneurs

What sets successful entrepreneurs apart from the rest? Is it luck, talent, or some secret formula? The truth is, while every entrepreneur's journey is unique, there are certain characteristics and traits that tend to be common among those who thrive in the entrepreneurial world. Let's explore these qualities and see how they align with your own strengths and aspirations.

1. Passion and Purpose:

    Successful entrepreneurs are driven by a deep passion for what they do. They have a burning desire to pursue their vision and make a meaningful impact. Passion fuels their motivation, determination, and resilience, allowing them to overcome obstacles and stay committed even when faced with challenges.

2. Resilience and Perseverance:

    Entrepreneurship is not a smooth ride. It's a rollercoaster of highs and lows, triumphs and setbacks. Successful entrepreneurs possess a resilient spirit that enables them to bounce back from failures, learn from their mistakes, and keep moving forward. They view challenges as opportunities for growth and see failure as a steppingstone toward success.

3. Creativity and Innovation:

    Entrepreneurs are often at the forefront of innovation. They possess a natural inclination to think outside the box, challenge the status quo, and find unique solutions to problems. They are willing to take risks and embrace uncertainty in order to bring their creative ideas to life.

4. Self-Discipline and Time Management:

   As an entrepreneur, you are your own boss. This requires a high level of self-discipline and effective time management skills. Successful entrepreneurs have the ability to prioritize tasks, set clear goals, and stay focused on what truly matters. They understand that their time is a valuable resource and allocate it wisely.

5. Strong Work Ethic:

   Building a successful business requires hard work and dedication. Successful entrepreneurs are willing to put in the effort, go the extra mile, and make sacrifices when needed. They have a strong work ethic and understand that success is not handed to them on a silver platter but is earned through perseverance and consistent action.

6. Adaptability and Flexibility:

   The entrepreneurial journey is full of surprises and unexpected twists. Successful entrepreneurs embrace change and are adaptable to evolving circumstances. They possess a flexible mindset that allows them to adjust their strategies, pivot when necessary, and seize new opportunities as they arise.

7. Continuous Learning:

   Entrepreneurs have a thirst for knowledge and a hunger for growth. They understand that learning is a lifelong process and actively seek opportunities to expand their skills and expertise. They read books, attend seminars, engage in networking, and surround themselves with mentors who can guide and inspire them.

Now, take a moment to reflect on these characteristics. Which ones resonate with you? Which ones do you already possess, and which ones do you aspire to develop further? Remember, entrepreneurship is a journey of self-discovery and growth, and you have the power to cultivate these qualities within yourself.

In the next section of this chapter, we'll explore the first steps you can take to answer the call of entrepreneurship. We'll discuss how to nurture the seed of an idea and begin transforming it into a viable business concept. Get ready to unleash your creativity, ignite your passion, and embark on an exciting journey of entrepreneurial exploration.

Are you feeling inspired? I hope so! Let's dive into Chapter 2: Nurturing the Seed of an Idea and discover how to bring your entrepreneurial dreams to life. It's time to turn your passion into a purpose-driven business.

Chapter 2: Nurturing the Seed of an Idea

Congratulations! You've taken the first step on your entrepreneurial journey by acknowledging your passion and desire for something more. Now, it's time to nurture the seed of an idea and begin transforming it into a viable business concept. Get ready to unleash your creativity, ignite your passion, and embark on an exciting journey of entrepreneurial exploration.

1. Identify Your Passion:

    The foundation of a successful business lies in your passion. What is it that truly excites and energizes you? What problems do you feel compelled to solve? Take some time to reflect on your interests, hobbies, and areas where you believe you can make a difference. Your passion will be the driving force that propels you through the challenges that lie ahead.

2. Research and Market Analysis:

    Once you've identified your passion, it's crucial to conduct thorough research and market analysis. Who are your potential customers? What are their needs and pain points? Is there a demand for the product or service you envision? Study the market landscape, identify your target audience, and gain a deep understanding of the competitive landscape. This knowledge will guide you in shaping your idea to meet market demands.

3. Refine Your Idea:

    As you gather insights from your research, it's time to refine your idea. Brainstorm different angles, consider innovative approaches, and seek feedback from trusted mentors or peers. Refining your idea involves clarifying your value proposition, identifying your unique selling points, and ensuring that your business idea aligns with your target market's needs.

4. Develop a Business Plan:

    A solid business plan is essential for guiding your entrepreneurial journey. It acts as a roadmap, outlining your goals, strategies, and financial projections. Consider aspects such as your business structure, marketing and sales strategies, operational processes, and financial projections. While your plan may evolve over time, having a blueprint will provide you with clarity and direction.

5. Validate Your Idea:

   Before fully committing to your business concept, it's crucial to validate it in the real world. Test your ideas through market research, surveys, and even pilot programs or prototypes. Seek feedback from potential customers, industry experts, and mentors. This validation process will help you refine your concept, identify potential challenges, and make informed decisions moving forward.

6. Build Your Support Network:

   Surrounding yourself with like-minded individuals who share your passion and entrepreneurial spirit can greatly enhance your journey. Seek out networking opportunities, join entrepreneurial communities, and connect with mentors who can provide guidance and support. Collaborating and learning from others will accelerate your growth and expand your possibilities.

7. Take the Leap:

   With a refined idea, a solid business plan, and a supportive network, it's time to take the leap and turn your vision into reality. Embrace the fear and uncertainty that comes with entrepreneurship, for it is often a sign that you're stepping out of your comfort zone and onto a path of growth. Trust in your abilities, stay committed to your purpose, and be prepared to work hard as you embark on this transformative journey.

Remember, entrepreneurship is a dynamic and iterative process. As you progress, you may need to pivot, adapt, and refine your strategies. Embrace the journey with an open mind and a willingness to learn from both successes and failures. Each step forward will bring you closer to realizing your dreams.

In the next chapter, we'll delve deeper into the mindset required to overcome fear and doubt as you navigate the entrepreneurial landscape. Get ready to embrace the challenges, believe in yourself, and unleash your full potential as an entrepreneur.

Exciting times lie ahead! Get ready to step into Chapter 3: Embracing the Risk: Overcoming Fear and Doubt.

Chapter 3: Embracing the Risk: Overcoming Fear and Doubt

As an entrepreneur, taking risks is inevitable. However, fear and doubt can often hinder our ability to make bold decisions and take action. In this chapter, we'll explore strategies for overcoming fear and doubt and embracing the risks that come with entrepreneurship.

1. Reframe Your Mindset:

   The first step to overcoming fear and doubt is to reframe your mindset. Instead of viewing risks as potential failures, see them as opportunities for growth and learning. Remember, failures are merely feedback and can provide valuable insights that lead to future success.

2. Identify Your Triggers:

   Understanding what triggers your fear and doubt can help you prepare for and mitigate these emotions. It could be a fear of failure, a lack of self-confidence, or uncertainty about the future. Once you identify your triggers, develop strategies to address them head-on.

3. Build Self-Confidence:

   Confidence is a crucial ingredient for success in entrepreneurship. Celebrate your wins, no matter how small, and acknowledge your strengths and abilities. Seek out constructive feedback, surround yourself with positive influences, and take steps to improve your skills and knowledge.

4. Take Calculated Risks:

   While it's essential to embrace risks, it's equally important to take calculated risks. Analyze the potential risks and rewards, weigh the costs and benefits, and develop contingency plans. Taking calculated risks reduces the likelihood of failure and increases the chances of success.

5. Take Action:

Procrastination and indecisiveness can lead to inaction and missed opportunities. Take action, even if it's a small step forward. Momentum builds momentum, and taking action creates a sense of progress and accomplishment.

6. Learn from Failure:

   Failure is an inevitable part of entrepreneurship. Instead of dwelling on the negative, approach failures with a growth mindset. Analyze what went wrong, identify areas for improvement, and apply those lessons to future endeavors.

7. Surround Yourself with Support:

   Surrounding yourself with supportive and positive influences can greatly impact your ability to overcome fear and doubt. Seek out mentors, join entrepreneurial communities, and build a support network of friends and family who encourage and uplift you.

Overcoming fear and doubt is a process that requires self-awareness, resilience, and a growth mindset. By reframing your mindset, building self-confidence, taking calculated risks, taking action, learning from failure, and surrounding yourself with support, you can overcome fear and doubt and embrace the risks that come with entrepreneurship.

In the next chapter, we'll delve into the importance of resilience and perseverance in entrepreneurship. Get ready to learn strategies for bouncing back from setbacks and staying committed to your goals.

Chapter 4: The Power of Connection: Effective Communication and Networking for Entrepreneurship

As an entrepreneur, building and nurturing relationships is essential for success. In this chapter, we'll explore the power of effective communication and networking and provide strategies for leveraging them to propel your business forward.

1. Develop Clear and Concise Communication Skills:

   Effective communication starts with clear and concise messaging. Practice articulating your business's mission, vision, and goals in a way that's easy to understand and compelling to others. This will help you communicate your value proposition and differentiate yourself from competitors.

2. Build Authentic Relationships:

   Networking is not just about exchanging business cards and making small talk; it's about building authentic relationships. Focus on connecting with individuals who share your values and interests and who you genuinely want to get to know better. Nurture these relationships over time by staying in touch, providing value, and offering support.

3. Attend Industry Events and Conferences:

   Industry events and conferences are excellent opportunities to connect with like-minded individuals and learn about new trends and innovations. Be strategic in your approach, research the event beforehand, set goals for what you want to achieve, and follow up with new contacts afterward.

4. Leverage Social Media:

   Social media is a powerful tool for networking and building relationships. Use platforms like LinkedIn, Facebook, TikTok, Twitter, and Instagram to connect with industry leaders, participate in relevant conversations, and share valuable content. Remember, social media is a two-way conversation; engage with your followers and build relationships.

5. Offer Value to Your Network:

    Building strong relationships is not just about what others can do for you, but what you can do for them. Offer value to your network by sharing your expertise, providing feedback, or making introductions. By being a valuable resource, you'll build trust and credibility with your network.

6. Practice Active Listening:

    Effective communication is not just about talking; it's also about listening. Practice active listening by giving your full attention to the person you're speaking with, asking thoughtful questions, and clarifying any misunderstandings. Active listening shows that you value the other person's input and helps build stronger relationships.

7. Follow Up and Follow Through:

    Building relationships is not a one-time event; it's an ongoing process. Follow up with new contacts after networking events, send thank-you notes, and follow through on any commitments you've made. By showing that you're reliable and consistent, you'll build trust and credibility with your network.

Effective communication and networking skills are essential for building and nurturing relationships in entrepreneurship. By developing clear and concise communication skills, building authentic relationships, attending industry events and conferences, leveraging social media, offering value to your network, practicing active listening, and following up and following through, you'll build a strong network that will help propel your business forward.

In the next chapter, we'll explore the importance of time management and productivity in entrepreneurship. Get ready to learn strategies for optimizing your time, increasing productivity, and achieving your goals efficiently and effectively.

Chapter 5: Mastering Time Management: Boosting Productivity for Entrepreneurial Success

Time is a precious resource for entrepreneurs, and mastering time management is crucial for maximizing productivity and achieving your goals. In this chapter, we'll explore strategies for optimizing your time, increasing productivity, and finding the right balance in your entrepreneurial journey.

1. Set Clear Goals:

Start by setting clear and specific goals for your business and personal life. Define what success looks like for you and break down your goals into actionable steps. Having clarity about your objectives will help you prioritize and allocate your time effectively.

2. Prioritize Your Tasks:

   Not all tasks are created equal. Prioritize your tasks based on their importance and urgency. Focus on high-value activities that align with your goals and have the greatest impact on your business. Learn to say no to non-essential tasks that can distract you from your priorities.

3. Plan and Schedule:

   Take time to plan and schedule your activities. Use productivity tools, such as calendars and task management apps, to organize your tasks and allocate specific time blocks for different activities. By having a clear plan, you'll minimize distractions and stay focused on your priorities.

4. Practice Time Blocking:

   Time blocking is a powerful technique for managing your time effectively. Dedicate specific blocks of time for different types of tasks, such as focused work, meetings, and breaks. This allows you to maintain a structured schedule and ensures that you allocate time for both important tasks and self-care.

5. Delegate and Outsource:

As an entrepreneur, it's essential to recognize that you can't do everything on your own. Delegate tasks that can be handled by others, whether it's hiring employees or outsourcing certain functions. This frees up your time to focus on strategic activities that require your expertise.

6. Avoid Multitasking:

    Multitasking may seem like a time-saver, but it can actually hinder productivity. Instead, practice single tasking by focusing on one task at a time. This allows you to give your full attention and energy to each task, resulting in better quality work and faster completion times.

7. Take Breaks and Rest:

    It's important to recharge and avoid burnout. Schedule regular breaks throughout your day to rest and rejuvenate. Stepping away from work can actually enhance productivity by giving your mind a chance to relax and recharge. Remember, taking care of yourself is essential for long-term success.

8. Learn to Say No:

    It's tempting to take on every opportunity that comes your way, but saying yes to everything can spread you too thin. Learn to say no to tasks, projects, or commitments that don't align with your goals or values. By setting boundaries, you'll have more time and energy for what truly matters.

9. Continuously Improve and Adapt:

Keep evaluating and refining your time management strategies. Reflect on what works for you and what doesn't and make adjustments as needed. The entrepreneurial journey is a learning process, and being open to continuous improvement will help you optimize your productivity over time.

By implementing these time management strategies, you'll be able to make the most of your time, increase productivity, and find a healthy balance in your entrepreneurial journey. Remember, time is a valuable asset, and how you manage it can greatly impact your success and overall well-being.

In the next chapter, we'll explore the importance of innovation and adaptability in entrepreneurship. Get ready to unleash your creativity, embrace change, and stay ahead of the curve in the ever-evolving business landscape.

Chapter 6: Unleashing Creativity: The Power of Innovation and Adaptability

Innovation and adaptability are the driving forces behind successful entrepreneurship. In this chapter, we'll explore the importance of unleashing your creativity, embracing change, and staying ahead of the curve in the ever-evolving business landscape.

1. Embrace a Growth Mindset:

A growth mindset is the belief that you can develop and improve your abilities through dedication and hard work. Embrace the mindset that you are capable of creativity and innovation. Believe that you can learn new skills, adapt to change, and come up with unique solutions to challenges.

2. Foster a Creative Environment:

Create an environment that encourages and nurtures creativity. Surround yourself with diverse perspectives, engage in brainstorming sessions, and foster a culture of open communication and idea-sharing. Encourage your team members to think outside the box and explore new possibilities.

3. Embrace Change as an Opportunity:

Change is inevitable in the business world. Rather than resisting change, embrace it as an opportunity for growth and improvement. Stay informed about industry trends, technological advancements, and consumer preferences. Be willing to adapt your strategies and business model to stay relevant and competitive.

4. Continuously Seek Knowledge:

Stay curious and invest in your own learning and development. Read books, attend seminars and workshops, and engage in conversations with experts in your field. The more knowledge and insights you gain, the better equipped you'll be to innovate and adapt to changes in the market.

5. Encourage Experimentation:

   Create a culture that embraces experimentation and risk-taking. Encourage yourself and your team members to try new approaches, even if they involve a level of uncertainty. Foster an environment where failures are seen as valuable learning opportunities rather than as reasons to give up.

6. Emphasize Customer-Centric Innovation:

   Innovate with your customers in mind. Listen to their feedback, understand their needs, and identify pain points that your business can address. By focusing on customer-centric innovation, you'll create products and services that truly resonate with your target audience.

7. Foster Collaboration and Partnerships:

   Collaboration with other individuals and businesses can spark new ideas and opportunities. Seek out partnerships that complement your strengths and bring fresh perspectives to the table. Collaborative efforts can lead to innovative solutions and expand your reach in the market.

8. Stay Agile and Flexible:

   In a fast-paced business environment, being agile and flexible is crucial. Be willing to pivot your strategies, adapt to new circumstances, and seize emerging opportunities. Maintain a mindset of continuous improvement and be ready to adjust your course as needed.

9. Celebrate and Learn from Successes and Failures:

   Celebrate your successes and learn from your failures. Recognize and acknowledge the accomplishments of yourself and your team members. Similarly, reflect on your failures and identify lessons that can inform future decisions and actions. Both successes and failures contribute to your growth as an entrepreneur.

By unleashing your creativity, embracing change, and staying ahead of the curve, you'll position yourself and your business for long-term success. Remember, innovation and adaptability are not reserved for a select few but can be cultivated and honed by anyone with the right mindset and approach.

In the next chapter, we'll explore the importance of resilience and perseverance in the face of adversity. Get ready to learn strategies for bouncing back from setbacks and staying committed to your entrepreneurial journey.

Chapter 7: The Power of Resilience: Bouncing Back and Thriving in Adversity

As an entrepreneur, you'll inevitably face challenges and setbacks along your journey. The key to success lies in your ability to bounce back, adapt, and thrive in the face of adversity. In this chapter, we'll explore the power of resilience and provide strategies for developing and nurturing this essential trait.

1. Embrace a Positive Mindset:

   Maintaining a positive mindset is crucial when facing adversity. Choose to see challenges as opportunities for growth and learning. Believe in your ability to overcome obstacles and stay optimistic about the future. A positive mindset will fuel your resilience and help you find solutions in the midst of adversity.

2. Cultivate Self-Compassion:

   Be kind and compassionate towards yourself during difficult times. Recognize that setbacks are a normal part of the entrepreneurial journey. Treat yourself with understanding, forgiveness, and patience. By cultivating self-compassion, you'll strengthen your resilience and bounce back stronger.

3. Seek Support from Your Network:

   Reach out to your support network during challenging times. Surround yourself with people who believe in you and can provide guidance, encouragement, and emotional support. Lean on your mentors, friends, and family for strength and reassurance. Remember, you don't have to face adversity alone.

4. Focus on Solutions, not Problems:

   When faced with adversity, shift your focus from the problem to potential solutions. Take a proactive approach and brainstorm different strategies to overcome the obstacle. By focusing on solutions, you'll feel empowered and motivated to take action.

5. Practice Adaptability:

   Adaptability is the ability to adjust and thrive in changing circumstances. Embrace change as an opportunity for growth and innovation. Be willing to pivot your strategies, explore new approaches, and take calculated risks. Adaptability will help you navigate unexpected challenges and emerge stronger.

6. Learn from Setbacks:

   View setbacks as valuable learning experiences. Reflect on what went wrong, identify lessons learned, and apply those insights to future endeavors. Embrace a growth mindset and see setbacks as steppingstones towards future success. By learning from setbacks, you'll continuously improve and become more resilient.

7. Take Care of Your Well-being:

   Prioritize your physical, mental, and emotional well-being during challenging times. Engage in activities that recharge and rejuvenate you, such as exercise, meditation, spending time with loved ones, or pursuing hobbies. Taking care of yourself strengthens your resilience and equips you to face adversity head-on.

8. Celebrate Small Victories:

   Celebrate even the smallest victories along your entrepreneurial journey. Recognize and appreciate progress, no matter how insignificant it may seem. Celebrating small wins boosts your motivation, confidence, and resilience. It reminds you of your capability to overcome challenges and succeed.

9. Stay Committed to Your Purpose:

   During tough times, reconnect with your purpose and the reasons why you embarked on your entrepreneurial journey. Remind yourself of the impact you want to make, the goals you've set, and the vision you have for your business. Your purpose will fuel your resilience and give you the strength to persevere.

By embracing resilience and implementing these strategies, you'll not only bounce back from setbacks but also thrive in the face of adversity. Remember, challenges are temporary roadblocks that can lead to even greater achievements. Stay resilient, stay determined, and keep moving forward.

In the next chapter, we'll explore the importance of effective decision-making and problem-solving skills in entrepreneurship. Get ready to learn strategies for making informed decisions and tackling complex problems with confidence.

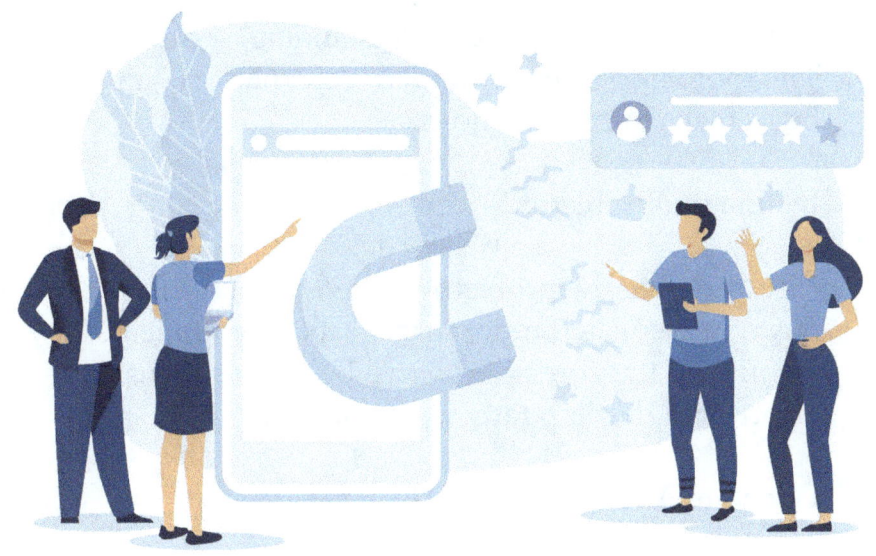

Chapter 8: Decisive Action: Making Informed Decisions and Solving Problems with Confidence

As an entrepreneur, you'll encounter countless decisions and complex problems that require your attention. The ability to make informed decisions and solve problems with confidence is essential for your success. In this chapter, we'll explore strategies for effective decision-making and problem-solving that will empower you to take decisive action.

1. Gather Relevant Information:

   Before making any decision or attempting to solve a problem, gather as much relevant information as possible. Conduct research, seek expert opinions, and analyze data to gain a comprehensive understanding of the situation. The more information you have, the better equipped you'll be to make informed choices.

2. Define the Problem:

   Clearly define the problem you're trying to solve. Break it down into smaller, more manageable components. By identifying the core issue, you'll be able to focus your efforts and develop targeted solutions.

3. Generate Alternatives:

   Brainstorm multiple alternatives and potential solutions. Encourage creativity and think outside the box. Don't limit yourself to the obvious choices. Consider both traditional and innovative approaches that align with your goals.

4. Evaluate Pros and Cons:

   Assess the potential benefits and drawbacks of each alternative. Consider the short-term and long-term implications, the feasibility of implementation, and the potential risks involved. This evaluation will help you make a balanced and informed decision.

5. Seek Input from Others:

   Don't hesitate to seek input from trusted advisors, mentors, or team members. Their perspectives and insights can shed light on aspects you may have overlooked. Collaboration and diverse viewpoints can lead to more robust solutions.

6. Trust Your Intuition:

   While gathering information and seeking input is crucial, don't discount the power of your intuition. Trust your instincts and listen to your gut feeling. Sometimes, your intuition can guide you towards the right decision when all the facts are unclear.

7. Analyze the Consequences:

   Consider the potential consequences of each decision or solution. Assess the impact on your business, stakeholders, and long-term goals. Strive for outcomes that align with your values and support the overall growth and sustainability of your venture.

8. Take Calculated Risks:

   Entrepreneurship inherently involves taking risks. Assess the level of risk associated with each decision and be willing to take calculated risks when necessary. Evaluate the potential rewards and weigh them against the potential drawbacks. Trust yourself and be willing to step outside your comfort zone.

9. Take Decisive Action:

   Once you've evaluated your options and considered the potential outcomes, it's time to take decisive action. Avoid analysis paralysis and embrace a bias towards action. Trust in your decision-making process and have confidence in your ability to adapt and course-correct along the way.

10. Reflect and Learn:

   After implementing your decision or solution, take time to reflect and evaluate the results. Learn from the outcomes, whether they are positive or negative. Use this knowledge to refine your decision-making and problem-solving skills for future challenges.

By employing these strategies, you'll develop the ability to make informed decisions and solve problems with confidence. Remember, decision-making and problem-solving are skills that can be honed through practice and experience. Embrace the challenges, trust your abilities, and take decisive action to propel your entrepreneurial journey forward.

In the next chapter, we'll explore the importance of effective leadership and building a high-performing team. Get ready to learn strategies for inspiring and motivating your team members to achieve collective success.

Chapter 9: Leading with Inspiration: Building a High-Performing Team for Collective Success

As an entrepreneur, one of your most critical responsibilities is building and leading a high-performing team. Your team members are the backbone of your business, and their collective efforts will determine the level of success you can achieve. In this chapter, we'll explore strategies for effective leadership that inspire and motivate your team towards collective success.

1. Lead by Example:

   As a leader, your actions speak louder than words. Set the standard by demonstrating the qualities and behaviors you expect from your team. Show integrity, work ethic, and a commitment to excellence. Your team will be inspired by your example and strive to emulate your dedication.

2. Communicate Vision and Purpose:

   Clearly communicate your vision and the purpose behind your business. Help your team members understand the impact of their work and how it aligns with the larger goals. When individuals feel connected to a meaningful purpose, they become more motivated and engaged.

3. Foster a Positive and Supportive Environment:

   Create a positive and supportive work environment where team members feel valued, respected, and empowered. Encourage open communication, collaboration, and idea-sharing. Celebrate successes, provide constructive feedback, and offer support when challenges arise. When individuals feel supported, they are more likely to give their best and contribute to the team's success.

4. Develop Trust and Empowerment:

   Trust is the foundation of a high-performing team. Build trust by being transparent, keeping your commitments, and empowering team members to make decisions and take ownership of their work. Trust fosters a sense of autonomy and encourages individuals to take the initiative and bring their best ideas to the table.

5. Recognize and Appreciate Achievements:

   Recognize and appreciate the achievements of your team members regularly. Celebrate milestones, both big and small. Acknowledge the individual contributions and the collective efforts that lead to success. Recognition and appreciation create a positive work culture and motivate team members to continue excelling.

6. Provide Growth and Development Opportunities:

   Invest in the growth and development of your team members. Offer training, mentorship, and opportunities for professional advancement. Support their goals and provide challenging projects that allow them to expand their skills and knowledge. When individuals see a path for growth within the team, they are more likely to stay motivated and committed.

7. Foster Collaboration and Teamwork:

   Encourage collaboration and teamwork within your team. Create opportunities for cross-functional collaboration and encourage individuals to learn from one another. Foster a sense of camaraderie and promote a "we" mentality, where team members support and uplift each other. When individuals work together towards a common goal, the team's performance and synergy are enhanced.

8. Encourage Innovation and Creativity:

   Foster a culture of innovation and creativity within your team. Encourage individuals to think outside the box, explore new ideas, and take calculated risks. Provide a safe space for experimentation and learning from failures. By fostering innovation, you'll unlock the team's potential and discover new solutions and opportunities.

9. Foster Work-Life Balance:

   Recognize the importance of work-life balance and support your team members in achieving it. Encourage them to prioritize self-care, maintain a healthy work-life integration, and recharge outside of work. When individuals feel balanced and fulfilled, their performance and commitment to the team are enhanced.

10. Lead with Empathy and Emotional Intelligence:

    Develop your emotional intelligence and lead with empathy. Understand and empathize with the challenges and aspirations of your team members. Be attentive to their needs, provide support during difficult times, and demonstrate genuine care for their well-being. Leading with empathy builds strong relationships and fosters a sense of belonging within the team.

By implementing these strategies, you'll create a high-performing team that is inspired, motivated, and committed to collective growth.

In the next chapter we dive into "Embracing Adaptability: Navigating Change and Thriving in a Dynamic Business Landscape.

Chapter 10: Embracing Adaptability: Navigating Change and Thriving in a Dynamic Business Landscape

In the fast-paced world of entrepreneurship, change is a constant. To succeed and thrive, you must embrace adaptability and navigate the ever-evolving business landscape with agility and optimism. In this chapter, we'll explore the power of adaptability and provide strategies for embracing change and turning it into a catalyst for growth.

1. Embrace a Growth Mindset:

Adopt a growth mindset that welcomes challenges and sees them as opportunities for learning and development. Believe in your ability to adapt and evolve in the face of change. Embracing a growth mindset allows you to approach new situations with optimism and resilience.

2. Stay Ahead of Trends:

   Stay informed about industry trends and market shifts. Regularly assess the competitive landscape and identify emerging opportunities. By staying ahead of trends, you can proactively adapt your business strategies to capitalize on new developments.

3. Foster a Culture of Innovation:

   Encourage innovation within your team and foster an environment that values creativity and out-of-the-box thinking. Encourage experimentation and provide the resources and support necessary for innovative ideas to flourish. Embracing innovation enables you to adapt and stay ahead of the curve.

4. Develop Continuous Learning Habits:

   Commit to lifelong learning and personal development. Stay curious and seek opportunities to expand your knowledge and skills. Encourage your team members to do the same. Continuous learning keeps you adaptable and equips you with the tools to navigate change effectively.

5. Build a Flexible Infrastructure:

   Create a flexible and scalable infrastructure that can easily adapt to changing circumstances. Invest in technologies and systems that support agility and allow for quick adjustments when needed. A flexible infrastructure enables you to respond swiftly to market shifts and customer demands.

6. Foster Open Communication:

   Establish a culture of open communication where team members feel comfortable sharing their ideas, concerns, and suggestions. Encourage transparent and honest conversations that promote collaboration and problem-solving. Effective communication helps the team adapt collectively to change.

7. Develop Cross-Functional Skills:

   Encourage your team members to develop cross-functional skills that enable them to contribute in various areas. This versatility enhances their adaptability and allows for smoother transitions during times of change. Cross-functional skills also foster a collaborative and agile team dynamic.

8. Seek Feedback and Iterate:
   Embrace feedback as a valuable tool for growth and improvement. Regularly seek feedback from customers, team members, and mentors. Use this feedback to iterate and refine your strategies. Adaptation requires a willingness to adjust based on feedback and evolving needs.

9. Embrace Strategic Partnerships:

    Collaborate with strategic partners who can complement your strengths and fill gaps in your expertise. Strategic partnerships provide access to new resources, networks, and knowledge. They can also offer support during periods of change and help navigate unfamiliar territory.

10. Foster Resilience and Positive Mindset:

    Develop resilience and maintain a positive mindset when faced with challenges and setbacks. Adaptability requires the ability to bounce back from adversity and see setbacks as temporary roadblocks, rather than insurmountable barriers. Cultivate resilience and optimism to navigate change with grace.

By embracing adaptability and implementing these strategies, you'll be well-equipped to navigate the ever-changing business landscape. Remember, change can be a catalyst for growth and innovation. Embrace it with optimism, learn from it, and use it as an opportunity to propel your business forward.

In the next chapter, we'll explore the importance of effective communication and relationship-building skills in entrepreneurship. Get ready to learn strategies for building strong connections, networking effectively, and fostering meaningful relationships that contribute to your success.

Chapter 11: The Power of Connection: Effective Communication and Relationship-Building for Entrepreneurial Success

In the world of entrepreneurship, effective communication and relationship-building skills are essential for success. Building strong connections, networking effectively, and fostering meaningful relationships can open doors to new opportunities, collaborations, and support. In this chapter, we'll explore the power of connection and provide strategies for enhancing your communication skills and building relationships that contribute to your entrepreneurial journey.

1. Active Listening:

   Develop the skill of active listening. When engaging in conversations, give your full attention, maintain eye contact, and show genuine interest in what the other person is saying. Listen not only to the words but also to the underlying emotions and messages being conveyed. Active listening allows you to establish a deeper connection with others and understand their needs and perspectives.

2. Clear and Concise Communication:

   Master the art of clear and concise communication. Express your ideas and thoughts in a way that is easy to understand. Avoid jargon or technical terms that may confuse others. Use simple language and provide relevant examples to illustrate your points. Clear communication fosters understanding and minimizes misinterpretation.

3. Non-Verbal Communication:

   Pay attention to your non-verbal cues. Your body language, facial expressions, and gestures convey a wealth of information. Maintain an open posture, smile genuinely, and use appropriate hand movements to enhance your message. Non-verbal communication can help establish rapport and build trust.

4. Storytelling:

   Harness the power of storytelling to connect with others on an emotional level. Share compelling stories that illustrate your values, experiences, and the journey behind your entrepreneurial venture. Stories create a personal connection and make your message memorable.

5. Networking with Authenticity:

   Approach networking with authenticity and a genuine interest in others. Instead of focusing solely on what you can gain, seek to build meaningful connections by understanding others' needs and offering support and assistance. Networking is about building mutually beneficial relationships that go beyond transactional exchanges.

6. Building an Online Presence:

   Leverage the power of digital platforms to build your online presence. Create a professional website, establish a strong presence on social media, and engage with your audience. Share valuable content, offer insights, and participate in relevant online communities. An online presence expands your reach and allows you to connect with a broader network of individuals.

7. Nurturing Relationships:

   Building relationships is an ongoing process. Take the time to nurture and maintain your connections. Stay in touch with your network through regular communication, whether it's a simple check-in, sharing relevant resources, or offering support. Show genuine care and interest in the well-being of others.

8. Collaboration and Partnerships:

   Seek opportunities for collaboration and partnerships. Identify individuals or organizations whose goals align with yours and explore ways to work together. Collaboration not only expands your network but also allows you to leverage the strengths and expertise of others.

9. Building a Supportive Community:

   Surround yourself with a supportive community of like-minded individuals. Join industry associations, attend networking events, and participate in entrepreneurial communities. Engage in meaningful conversations, share experiences, and seek advice and support when needed. A supportive community can provide guidance, inspiration, and opportunities for collaboration.

10. Emotional Intelligence:

    Develop your emotional intelligence to better understand and navigate interpersonal dynamics. Be aware of your own emotions and how they impact your interactions. Show empathy and consider the emotions of others. Emotional intelligence allows you to build stronger relationships and resolve conflicts effectively.

By honing your communication skills and building meaningful relationships, you'll create a strong foundation for entrepreneurial success. Remember, entrepreneurship is not a solitary journey but one that thrives on connections and collaborations. Embrace the power of connection, communicate effectively, and foster relationships that contribute to your growth and fulfillment.

In the next chapter, we'll explore the importance of lifelong learning and fueling your growth in an ever changing landscape.

Chapter 12: Lifelong Learning: Fueling Growth and Adapting to a Changing Business Landscape

In the dynamic world of entrepreneurship, the pursuit of knowledge and continuous learning is a never-ending journey. To stay ahead in a rapidly evolving business landscape, it's crucial to embrace lifelong learning and invest in your personal growth. In this final chapter, we'll explore the importance of continuous learning and provide strategies for expanding your knowledge, honing your skills, and adapting to the ever-changing demands of entrepreneurship.

1. Embrace a Curious Mindset:

   Cultivate a curiosity for learning and a thirst for knowledge. Approach each day as an opportunity to explore new ideas, concepts, and industry trends. Ask questions, seek answers, and never stop being curious. Embracing a curious mindset fuels your growth and keeps you adaptable.

2. Read Widely:

   Make reading a regular habit and explore a diverse range of topics. Read books, articles, blogs, and industry publications that expand your understanding of entrepreneurship, business strategies, and emerging trends. Reading widens your perspective and exposes you to new ideas and insights.

3. Attend Workshops and Conferences:

   Take advantage of workshops, seminars, and conferences in your industry. These events provide opportunities to learn from experts, gain practical knowledge, and network with like-minded individuals. Engage in discussions, ask questions, and actively participate to maximize your learning experience.

4. Seek Mentorship:

   Find mentors who can guide you on your entrepreneurial journey. Look for experienced individuals who have achieved success in your field of interest. Their insights, advice, and support can prove invaluable as you navigate challenges and seek opportunities for growth.

5. Online Learning and Courses:

   Leverage the abundance of online learning platforms and courses available. Enroll in courses that enhance your skills, expand your knowledge, and address specific areas of interest. Online learning provides flexibility and allows you to learn at your own pace.

6. Embrace New Technologies:

   Stay updated with emerging technologies relevant to your industry. Embrace digital tools and platforms that can streamline your processes, improve efficiency, and enhance your competitive edge. Being technologically savvy positions you well in a rapidly evolving business landscape.

7. Network and Collaborate:

   Engage in networking activities to connect with professionals in your industry. Attend industry events, join entrepreneurial communities, and participate in online forums. Building a strong network allows you to exchange knowledge, gain insights, and collaborate on projects that fuel your growth.

8. Reflect and Evaluate:

   Take time to reflect on your experiences, both successes, and failures. Evaluate what worked well and what could have been done differently. Continuous self-reflection helps identify areas for improvement and informs your future actions.

9. Embrace Feedback:

   Seek feedback from customers, mentors, and peers. Be open to constructive criticism and use it as an opportunity for growth. Feedback provides valuable insights into areas where you can refine your skills and enhance your entrepreneurial journey.

10. Foster a Growth Mindset:

    Cultivate a growth mindset that believes in your ability to learn, adapt, and evolve. Embrace challenges as opportunities for growth rather than obstacles. Embracing a growth mindset enables you to approach learning with enthusiasm and resilience.

By embracing continuous learning and personal growth, you position yourself for long-term success as an entrepreneur. The journey doesn't end here—rather, it is a lifelong pursuit of knowledge, skills, and personal development. Stay curious, be open to new experiences, and embrace learning as a fundamental aspect of your entrepreneurial journey.

Congratulations! You've reached the end of this book, "Entrepreneurial Mindset-Do YOU Have What It Takes?" Throughout these chapters, we have explored various aspects of the entrepreneurial mindset and provided strategies for embracing entrepreneurship with optimism and resilience.

Being an entrepreneur is not just about starting a business; it's a mindset and a way of life. It's about embracing the freedom to create, innovate, and make a meaningful impact in the world. As you embark on your entrepreneurial journey, remember that you have what it takes to succeed. You possess unique skills, talents, and ideas that can shape the future.

The road ahead may have its ups and downs, but that's all part of the adventure. Embrace challenges as opportunities for growth and learning. Believe in your abilities, trust your instincts, and never be afraid to take calculated risks. Remember, failure is not the end; it's a steppingstone towards success.

Surround yourself with a supportive network of mentors, friends, and fellow entrepreneurs who can provide guidance and encouragement along the way. Seek inspiration from stories of other successful entrepreneurs who have faced similar challenges and triumphed against all odds.

Stay focused on your vision and goals, but also remain adaptable in a world that is constantly evolving. Embrace change and embrace new technologies and strategies that can propel your business forward. Stay connected to your customers and listen to their needs. Be willing to pivot, iterate, and innovate as you strive to meet their expectations.

Never underestimate the power of collaboration. Look for opportunities to partner with like-minded individuals and businesses that share your values and complement your strengths. Together, you can achieve more and create a positive impact that extends beyond your own ventures.

Celebrate every milestone along the way, no matter how small. Each step forward is a testament to your resilience and determination. Take time to reflect on your achievements and the progress you've made. Celebrate your wins and use them as fuel to keep pushing forward.

Remember, being an entrepreneur is a journey, not a destination. Enjoy the process, savor the victories, and learn from the setbacks. Embrace the opportunity to work for yourself, to pursue your passion, and to make a difference in the lives of others.

So, are you ready to embark on this incredible adventure? Embrace the entrepreneur mindset, believe in yourself, and let your passion guide you. The possibilities are endless, and the world is waiting for your unique contributions. Get out there, make your mark, and create a future that is truly extraordinary.

Wishing you all the success and fulfillment on your entrepreneurial journey!

Sincerely and with love for all making their mark on our collective world, Go Get 'Em!
Liane Pinel
https://lianepinel.com

www.ingramcontent.com/pod-product-compliance
Lightning Source LLC
Chambersburg PA
CBHW072207170526
45158CB00004BB/1795